Warning:

The content of this book is based solely on advice and opinions. In the event of any emergency or situation that poses a threat to any person, animal, or object, it is crucial to immediately contact the appropriate and specialized authorities for the situation, such as the police, firefighters, doctors... and follow all their specifications.

Original Title: Surviving the Unthinkable: Survival Guide.

© Surviving the Unthinkable: Survival Guide, Carlos Martínez Cerdá and Víctor Martínez Cerdá, 2023

Authors: Víctor Martínez Cerdá and Carlos Martínez Cerdá (V&C Brothers)

© Cover and illustrations: V&C Brothers

Layout and design: V&C Brothers

SURVIVING THE UNTHINKABLE

SURVIVAL GUIDE

1

Are they following me?

If you think a car or person is following you, make a right turn 4 times, on the corners of the streets you come across.

By turning right 4 times, you will return to your starting point.

If the person is still behind you, then they are truly following you.

However, it's important to note that this technique is not 100% effective and shouldn't be considered a definitive solution if you feel you're being followed.

If someone believes they are being followed, it's recommended that they try to find a safe place and call the police.

It's also important to be aware of your surroundings and try to note any relevant information, such as a description of the person or vehicle you believe is following you.

2

Physical Assault.

If you are subjected to a mugging, sexual assault, rape..., it's advised to scratch the attacker as much as possible.

Their DNA will remain under your nails, and later it can be used to identify them.

It's important to emphasize that if you are in a situation of physical assault, your priority should be to protect your physical well-being and seek help immediately.

If you're in danger, call the police or your local emergency services.

Regarding the suggestion of scratching the attacker to obtain their DNA, this can be useful in some cases to identify the assailant, but it's not always feasible.

In situations of aggression, your priority might be to escape or defend yourself, and you might not be able to collect evidence at that time.

Furthermore, just because an attacker's DNA is found under your nails doesn't necessarily mean the police will be able to identify them.

The most important thing in the case of physical assault is to seek help and support from trained professionals who can assist you in processing the trauma and pursuing legal action if necessary.

Seek help from the police, a doctor, a therapist, a support group, or any other organization that can help you overcome the situation in a safe and healthy manner.

3

Where to Hide in Case of Armed Conflict?

When caught in a situation involving light weapons combat, the ideal hiding spot would be in a protected area such as a bathtub or a concrete container.

When this isn't feasible, you should lie down and cover yourself with objects that can shield you from both debris and bullets.

It's crucial to stay away from windows, as they can pose a threat if they shatter due to the force of explosions or bullet impact.

If necessary, objects like mattresses, pillows, blankets, or books can be used to create an additional protective barrier.

It's essential to remain quiet and avoid making unnecessary noise to not draw attention.

If there's a chance to communicate with the outside, try to seek help and request assistance as soon as possible.

In any situation, it's vital to stay calm and have an emergency action plan in place.

4

Cactus Water.

The only liquid you'll get from a cactus in the middle of the desert is a few drops of a greenish fluid, both bitter and spicy, that will likely make you vomit, causing even more dehydration.

There is a certain type of barrel cactus from which water can be extracted, but it's not easy to find.

For survival, it's more effective to search for rock depressions where morning dew might have condensed into a few drops or some moisture.

A good amount of water is the first thing you should bring with you to the woods, the desert, or similar environments.

5

Emergency Windows.

If you need to break a car, bus, or other vehicle window because you're trapped after an accident, don't attempt to break it in the center.

These windows are typically made of tempered glass, so they are much more fragile when struck at the edges.

That's where you should hit.

If you try to break the glass in the center, you might not succeed since tempered glass is very durable.

Moreover, striking the center of the glass may cause it to crack and create small fissures instead of shattering it entirely, further complicating an emergency exit.

Therefore, it's better to strike the window at the edges, where the glass is more vulnerable and can break more easily.

To do this, you can use any object at hand, like a rock, hammer, or a heavy object.

It's crucial to cover your eyes with your hands to protect yourself from flying shards of glass when breaking the window.

If possible, try to break the window on the side opposite of traffic to avoid being hit by moving vehicles.

Once you've broken the window, carefully exit the vehicle to avoid injury from the sharp edges of the broken glass.

6

Chemical Burns.

These are injuries to the skin and in some cases, deeper tissues, caused by contact with chemical substances.

These substances can include acids, alkalis, solvents, chlorine, among others.

Chemical burns can be very dangerous, as they can penetrate the body's tissues rapidly and cause damage.

In the event of a chemical burn, it is essential to take immediate action to minimize damage and pain.

Firstly, one should remove the clothing or object that came into contact with the chemical and wash the affected skin with lukewarm water and soap for at least 20 minutes.

Cold water or ice should not be applied to a chemical burn, as it can worsen the injury.

It's also crucial not to apply any creams or ointments to the affected skin, as this can trap the chemical in the skin and exacerbate the injury.

Immediate medical attention should be sought for any chemical burn, especially if it's extensive, covers a large area of the body, is near the eyes, mouth, or respiratory passages, or if the ingested chemical is toxic.

Medical treatment may include washing the skin, medications, bandaging, transfer to a burn center, among others.

7

Emergency Calls Without Coverage.

There is an agreement between mobile phone operators to allow the use of their networks in emergency situations, even if the caller is not a customer of the particular operator or doesn't have signal in that area.

This is because emergency calls are a priority and should be facilitated at all times.

If your phone does not have a signal, try moving to an area where you might get coverage or use a landline if possible.

It's also important to remember that emergency calls should only be used in real emergency situations.

Misusing them can jeopardize the lives of others who genuinely need help.

8

Sleep With The Door Closed.

It can be an important safety measure in case of emergencies, such as a fire or a gas leak.

This is because closing the door can prevent smoke, heat, and toxic gases from spreading throughout the house and confining them to a single room.

Furthermore, a closed door can slow the spread of the fire and provide more time to escape or find a safe exit.

It's important to note that while sleeping with the door closed can be a helpful safety measure, it can also have some downsides in terms of ventilation and temperature.

Therefore, it's recommended to have proper ventilation in the room and to keep the door closed only during the night or when away from home for an extended period.

It's also crucial to have smoke and carbon monoxide detectors installed in the home to quickly detect any emergencies.

9

Ask for Help.

It's important to know that in emergency situations, it's crucial to seek help as soon as possible.

If you're injured and need assistance, don't wait for someone to approach you; take the initiative and approach someone specific.

When asking for help, it's vital to be specific and clear about what you need, like calling emergency services or seeking first aid.

By addressing a specific person, they are more likely to feel engaged and assist you quicker.

If you're in a public place, like a park or a busy street, find someone nearby and ask for their help directly.

If no one is around, look for a place where you might find assistance, such as a business establishment or a police station.

It's essential not to assume someone else will seek help for you, as this can lead to delays in medical attention and worsen your health condition.

If you feel uncomfortable asking for help directly, you can call emergency services yourself or ask someone to do it for you.

In any case, the most important thing is to seek help as soon as possible and not wait for the situation to deteriorate.

10

Deep Wound.

If you have sustained a large, deep wound from a sharp object, it's recommended not to remove the object.

The reason is that the object might be acting as a plug, preventing blood from gushing out, and removing it could lead to severe bleeding.

Furthermore, in some cases, the object could be close to an artery, and its removal might rupture it, which could be potentially fatal.

Instead, it's essential to apply pressure around the wound to stop the bleeding.

If possible, elevate the affected limb to reduce blood flow and seek medical attention as soon as possible.

Healthcare professionals will know how to handle the wound safely and appropriately.

11

Useful Homemade Inventions.

-Homemade heater or lamp: Insert crumpled cardboard into a small metal box, and you can use it as a heater or lamp.

-Mosquito trap: If you're tired of getting bitten, mix water, brown sugar, and yeast in a container and place it away from where you are.

-Camping lamp: With a small headlamp and a water jug, you can create a lamp capable of lighting up your entire tent.

-Homemade cooler: Place a clay pot inside a larger one and fill the gap between the two with sand. Any food you put in the smaller pot will stay cooler.

-Fix a flat tire: In the event of a puncture, you can fill the tire with grass to continue on your way.

-Intruder alarm: A glow stick, a mouse trap, and a string are all you need to create an intruder alarm.

-A candle from vegetable shortening: Insert a wick into a jar of natural shortening for a long-lasting candle.

12

Drowning.

It's important to note that choking from drowning can be a serious issue and must be addressed quickly and effectively.

If someone is truly drowning, the following steps should be taken:

Call emergency services immediately for help.

If possible, try to get the person out of the water.

If they're in a pool or the sea, look for something you can use to help them get out, like a rope or a flotation device.

If the person is unconscious, start cardiopulmonary resuscitation (CPR) immediately.

If you don't know how, the emergency services will guide you over the phone until help arrives.

If the person is conscious but struggling to breathe, ask them to cough to try and expel whatever is blocking their throat.

If the person can't cough or if they are unconscious, perform the Heimlich maneuver, which involves applying abdominal pressure to try and force out the obstructing item.

It's essential to be prepared for emergency situations, especially when around or near water.

It is recommended to take first aid and CPR classes to be prepared in case of an emergency.

13

Ice.

It's important to note that walking on ice is always hazardous and should be done with caution.

If there is no urgent need to cross a frozen lake, it's best to avoid it entirely.

In the event that you fall into icy water, it's vital to remain calm and try to keep your head above water.

If you are alone, attempt to climb back onto the ice and move away from the hole you fell through, using your elbows and legs to distribute your weight and prevent breaking the ice further.

If someone is nearby, ask them to help you out by using an object such as a branch, rope, or coat.

Bear in mind that extremely low temperatures can cause hypothermia, even if you're wet for just a few minutes.

Therefore, after getting out of the water, it's best to seek shelter and change out of wet clothes into dry ones as quickly as possible.

If possible, seek medical attention as soon as possible to prevent complications.

14

Three signs of a heart attack or stroke.

How can you tell if someone is having a heart attack or stroke?

-Ask them to smile: If one side of their face droops, it's an attack.

-Ask them to raise both arms overhead: If they can't lift one, it's an attack.

-Ask them to repeat a simple sentence: If they can't or say strange things, it's an attack.

Other common signs of a heart attack may include chest pain or discomfort, shortness of breath, sweating, nausea or vomiting, and dizziness or lightheadedness.

On the other hand, stroke symptoms can include numbness or weakness in the face, arm, or leg (especially on one side of the body), difficulty speaking or understanding language, blurred or double vision, and dizziness or loss of balance or coordination.

If someone shows these symptoms, it's crucial to call emergency services immediately.

Furthermore, it's essential to understand that symptoms can vary depending on the individual and the type of attack, and some attacks may be silent or have milder symptoms.

15

False Myth: If you're lost, eat quickly for survival.

Although nutrition is essential for our health, if we're lost in the woods, there are more important things than eating.

Our bodies can survive up to 6 weeks without food, depending on each person's health condition.

The immediate priority is to find water and shelter.

16

Prisoner.

If someone grabs you by the wrists, the easiest way to break free is by the thumbs.

The reason? It's the least forceful finger.

In some self-defense techniques, it's taught that the thumbs are the best choice for escaping, as they are the strongest fingers and have a greater capacity for twisting and bending.

However, in other techniques, one might use the strength of the wrist and the overall body force to break free from the grip.

In any case, it's important to note that the best way to escape a hold is through regular practice of self-defense techniques and proper training in combat situations.

17

When it comes to sourcing water for survival in extreme situations, some of the most common options are:

-Surface waters: If you're in an area with rivers, streams, or lakes, you can try to source water from these bodies. It's important to remember that water from natural water bodies may be contaminated with bacteria, viruses, and other microorganisms. Therefore, it should be boiled or filtered before consumption.

-Rainwater: If you're in an area where it rains regularly, you can collect rainwater using containers or collecting materials. Ensure that the containers are clean before collecting the water and boil or filter the water before drinking.

-Plants: Some, like bamboo and vines, may contain water inside. You can also collect dew from plant leaves early in the morning.

-Groundwater: In some areas, you can find groundwater through springs or wells. However, it's important to note that groundwater might be contaminated and may need to be treated before drinking.

-Condensation: You can produce your own water through condensation. To do this, cover a container with a plastic bag or tarp and place a stone in the center to form a depression. Then, place a container beneath the stone and wait for water vapor to condense inside.

-Snow or ice: Care must be taken as this water will cause our body temperature to drop, in addition to consuming body heat. You can try boiling the snow over a fire, then let it cool down before drinking.

It's vital to remember that any water source found in the wild might be contaminated with harmful microorganisms and chemicals.

Therefore, it's essential to boil, filter, or treat the water before consumption to prevent illnesses and ensure your survival.

18

Surviving bear encounters.

It's a significant topic for those who spend time in wilderness areas where these animals live.

There are three bear species found in North America: the black bear, the brown bear, and the polar bear.

Each of them has its own behavior and response to humans, so it's crucial to know the specific survival strategies for each.

When encountering a bear, the first thing one should do is stay calm and avoid any behavior that might be perceived as threatening.

In general, it's better to keep a certain distance and make noise to alert the bear to our presence.

If the bear seems interested in us, the best course of action is to back away slowly without turning your back or running, as this can trigger an attack.

For black and brown bears, it's often recommended to make oneself appear larger, speak loudly, and make noise, even banging objects or waving branches to scare the bear and let it know we are not easy prey.

If the bear gets too close, bear pepper spray can be used as a defensive measure.

Regarding polar bears, it's advised to stay away, as they are more aggressive than black and brown bears.

If a polar bear approaches, it's essential to remain calm, avoid making noise, and avoid making eye contact.

In the event of an attack, one should use a firearm or bear pepper spray, though it's crucial to know how to use these defensive means effectively.

In general, if a bear attacks, one needs to be mentally prepared to fight for survival.

This might include shouting and hitting the bear with objects, even using hands and feet in self-defense.

19

Snakebites.

They are a potentially lethal medical emergency, and it's important to know how to respond properly in case of a bite.

Venomous snakes are found all over the world and, depending on the species, their venom can cause a wide range of symptoms, ranging from pain and swelling at the bite site to respiratory issues, organ failure, and death.

If bitten by a snake, it's crucial to immediately call emergency services or get to a medical facility as soon as possible.

On the way to the medical center, the bitten limb should be kept below the level of the heart to restrict blood flow to the affected area, thus slowing the spread of the venom.

It's vital to avoid physical activity or movements that might accelerate the circulation of the venom in the body.

Attempting to extract the venom using home remedies, such as making a cut at the affected site or trying to suck out the venom, is not recommended.

Not only are these methods ineffective, but they can also worsen the situation by increasing the risk of infection and spreading the venom.

Applying ice to the bite area is also not advised, as it can exacerbate swelling.

In some instances, a tourniquet can be used to reduce blood flow to the affected area.

However, it should only be used as a last resort in situations where the medical facility is far away, and it's believed the individual won't reach it in time for treatment.

The tourniquet should be placed above the bite but should never be too tight, as it can cut off blood flow and cause permanent tissue damage.

20

The idea of punching a shark in the nose as a defense method against an attack is a popular strategy, but its effectiveness is questionable.

While it's true that sharks have ampullae of Lorenzini sensors in their noses that allow them to detect prey, hitting them on the nose may not be enough to deter an aggressive shark.

In general, the best way to avoid a shark attack is to refrain from swimming in areas known for sharks and to heed warning signs on beaches.

If you're in the water and see a shark, it's important to remain calm and try to move away from the shark slowly, avoiding sudden movements that might trigger an aggressive response.

In the event of an attack, it's essential to remember that sharks generally do not want to harm humans, and many attacks are actually exploratory bites, where the shark bites to determine if the prey is edible or not.

In these situations, the goal is to make the shark realize that we aren't suitable prey.

To do this, it's advised to strike and kick the shark's nose and eyes, as these are its most sensitive areas.

One can also try hitting the shark's gills, as these can be painful and might cause the shark to retreat.

If you have an object at hand, like a stick or a surfboard, it can be used to fend off the shark.

It's important to remember that the best defense is prevention. Being aware of the risks when swimming in areas known for sharks and taking necessary precautions can significantly reduce the risk of an attack.

21

The myth that moss always grows on the north side of trees is false.

While it's true that moss tends to thrive in damp and shaded environments, its distribution on trees isn't solely based on cardinal direction.

Moss is a seedless plant that reproduces through spores, and its growth largely depends on environmental conditions such as moisture, temperature, light, and air quality.

In some places, moss may grow more on the north side of trees because it receives less direct sunlight, but this isn't a universal rule.

22

The "Triangle of Life" theory.

It is a misguided concept that has been debunked by experts in seismic safety and earthquake rescue.

The triangle of life refers to a supposedly safe space created by a triangle formed by a wall, ceiling, and a heavy object like furniture, in the event that the ceiling collapses during an earthquake.

However, the triangle of life theory is not backed by scientific evidence and is potentially dangerous, as it can lead people to seek shelter in inappropriate places during an earthquake.

In modern buildings, doors and walls are strong enough to withstand the impact of falling debris during an earthquake, and doorframes do not provide any significant additional protection.

Instead, seismic safety experts recommend the "Drop, Cover, and Hold On" method as the best way to protect oneself during an earthquake.

This involves dropping to the ground, covering one's head and neck with their arms, and seeking shelter under a sturdy and solid object, like a desk or table.

If there isn't such an object available, it's important to cover oneself with hands and find shelter in a place where one can avoid objects that might fall.

23

In emergency situations following an explosion, the most important thing is to move away from the explosion site as quickly as possible and seek shelter in a safe place, away from the affected area.

If there are injured individuals or urgent medical assistance is needed, emergency services should be called.

However, it's true that after an explosion, there's the possibility of a secondary explosive device intentionally placed to harm first responders and rescuers.

Therefore, caution is essential when calling emergency services, ensuring there isn't an imminent threat of a second explosion before doing so.

If there's a belief of a threat of a second explosion, it's important to wait in a safe place and seek assistance from law enforcement or emergency teams in person.

In any case, it's essential to follow instructions from authorities and emergency teams and remain vigilant for any signs of additional danger.

24

If a fire occurs in a device or appliance, it is important to take immediate measures to prevent the fire from spreading and turning into a larger emergency.

However, it's true that unplugging the device or dousing it with water can be extremely dangerous and increase the risk of electrocution.

Instead of trying to disconnect the affected device, it's crucial to move away from the area and call emergency services right away so they can respond and manage the situation.

If possible, turning off the automatic safety controller in the home's electrical panel can be a safe way to cut off power and prevent the fire from spreading.

It's important to remember that in the event of a fire, personal safety is the number one priority.

One should not risk their life or health in an attempt to save the device or property.

Instead, call emergency services and follow the instructions of firefighters and other first responders who arrive at the scene.

25

There are different ways to start a fire in the wild without the need for lighters or matches.

Some of the most common methods include:

-Friction: This technique involves rubbing two materials together to produce heat and create a spark that can ignite a fire. Some examples of materials that can be used include wood, bamboo, animal skin, and others.

-Lens: This technique relies on using a lens or glass to focus sunlight onto a single point to generate heat. You can use contact lenses, magnifying glasses, or even a water-filled bottle to create a magnifying effect.

-Striking: This technique involves striking two materials together to produce sparks. The materials that can be used include flint and steel, or even two hard stones.

-Bow and drill: This method involves using a bow and a drill to generate heat and start a fire. This technique requires some skill and practice, but it can be very effective if done correctly.

As for the materials needed, it will depend on the chosen technique.

For instance, for the friction method, you will need dry wood, a drill, and a bow, while for the lens method you will need a lens or glass, and for the striking method, you will need flint and steel or two hard stones.

It's important to note that, regardless of the method used, precautions should always be taken to prevent unwanted fires and to follow local rules and regulations related to outdoor burning.

26

David LaVau.

He is a person who had an incredible survival story after falling off a 60-meter cliff in California, United States.

LaVau fell while trying to dodge another car on a mountainous road, and was lost for 6 days before being found by his relatives.

During that time, LaVau had to survive with broken bones and a dislocated shoulder.

To find food, he ate insects and plant leaves, and drank water from nearby streams.

Despite his injuries and the lack of food and water, LaVau managed to survive until he was rescued.

David LaVau's survival case highlights the resilience and tenacity of the human spirit in extreme situations.

Even though his body was severely injured and weakened, his survival spirit allowed him to keep going and do everything possible to survive.

27

The amateur rugby team Old Christians, 1972.

A chartered plane from the Uruguayan Air Force was en route to Chile when it crashed in the Andes mountains, killing 12 of the 45 people on board.

Trapped on a snow-covered and isolated mountain, others soon succumbed to their injuries, the cold, or starvation, including 8 who perished in an avalanche.

When they ran out of food, some of them ate the flesh of the deceased, but one who refused to do so died of starvation.

The 16 survivors were rescued 72 days after the crash when two of them trekked across the mountains for 10 days to seek help in Chile.

28

Joe Simpson, 1985.

British mountaineers Joe Simpson and Simon Yates were climbing the 6,400-meter Siula Grande mountain in the Peruvian Andes when Simpson, at the age of 25, fell and broke his leg.

Yates, 21, spent a day trying to lower Simpson with a rope down to the base, but mistakenly ended up lowering him over a ledge.

Simpson was left hanging helplessly while Yates began to slip.

When Yates cut the rope to save his own life, Simpson dropped down the side of the mountain.

Trapped without water or food, crippled and suffering hallucinations from pain, Simpson still managed to climb out of the crevice and slowly make his way across rocky terrain, a glacier, around a lake, and into a rocky valley.

Three and a half days later, he reached camp.

He later wrote a book about his harrowing experience, Touching the Void, which was adapted into a film in 2003, winning several awards.

29

Aron Ralston, April 2003.

Featured in Danny Boyle's movie 127 Hours, Ralston was hiking alone in a remote canyon in Utah when a rock fell, pinning his arm.

The experienced hiker, aged 27, ran out of water 3 days later.

Another 2 days passed before he realized his only chance of survival would be a drastic measure: cutting off his own arm.

"First I was able to break the radius and, after a few minutes, the ulna at the wrist.

From there, I had the knife, applied the tourniquet, and proceeded to cut.

The process took about an hour," he said later.

He then descended to the bottom of the canyon, where he encountered other hikers.

Later on, park rangers used heavy equipment to move the 363-kilogram (800-pound) rock and recover Ralston's arm, which was taken to a morgue.

30

Colin Jones, an Australian miner, became trapped in a coal mine in June 2003 when his tractor overturned and crushed his arm against a wall.

Fearing that the tractor would explode before he could be rescued, Jones asked a colleague to amputate his arm, but he refused.

Desperate, Jones decided to do it himself with a short-bladed knife.

Finally, after several hours, he was rescued and taken to a hospital, where he was treated for his injuries.

His incredible act of survival and determination became an inspiring story for many and earned him the nickname "the one-armed man".

31

Daryl Jane.

It's a survival case under extreme conditions where a person managed to survive nearly two weeks in the forest under adverse weather conditions.

In December of 2006, while driving her Jeep near Mount Adams, she became trapped in snow on a remote path.

Jane had with her some supplies, such as water, rice cakes, and small snacks, but after rationing them for several days, she ran out of water and had to resort to drinking from puddles.

Jane showed a great ability to adapt to the situation and used her ingenuity to survive, such as building a shelter with branches and snow, and making a fire to keep warm.

She also sought help, leaving signs and hints for rescue teams that might be looking for her.

Despite the low temperatures, Jane managed to avoid frostbite and maintained her physical and mental health throughout the two weeks she was lost.

Daryl Jane's case is an example of how perseverance and the ability to adapt to extreme situations can make a difference in a survival situation.

Furthermore, it's important to emphasize the significance of carrying appropriate supplies and knowing how to use them in case of an emergency.

It's also crucial to stay calm and actively seek help if found in a similar situation.

32

Soccer Players in the Gulf of Mexico, February 2009.

4 athletes, including 2 American soccer players, fell into the water in the Gulf of Mexico, 75 miles off the coast, when their fishing boat capsized.

The boat flipped when its owner revved the engine, trying to free a stuck anchor.

Initially, the men remained calm, even as darkness fell and a storm approached, clinging to the overturned hull.

After almost two days, amidst waves up to 15 feet high, they began to shake violently and hallucinate, as one by one they succumbed to delirium, hypothermia, and exhaustion.

Only Nick Schuyler, a personal trainer, survived.

33

Jamie Neale.

He is a British hiker who in July 2009 got lost for 12 days in the Blue Mountains of Australia, west of Sydney.

Neale had strayed off the path and become disoriented, leading him to get lost in the dense mountain vegetation.

Despite the efforts of rescue teams, who used helicopters to search for him, Neale wasn't found and had to survive on his own.

He sustained himself on a diet of berries and other wild foods he found in nature and sheltered with tree bark to protect himself from the cold at night.

Finally, after 12 days, Neale was discovered by two soldiers who were hiking in the area and heard his calls for help.

Although he was dehydrated and malnourished, Neale survived his mountain ordeal and made a full recovery.

Since then, he has given motivational talks and written a book about his survival experience.

34

Amos Wayne Richards.

He is a survivor who broke his leg and dislocated his shoulder after falling while hiking alone in a Utah desert in September 2011.

He only had 2 protein bars to eat, so he set his shoulder and began to crawl across the terrain towards his car.

To stay hydrated, he collected rainwater in a bottle and managed to slowly cover five miles.

After four days, he was found by rescuers searching for him in a helicopter, who treated his leg injury and dehydration.

This is an example of how determination and the ability to improvise can be key in survival situations.

35

On March 11, 2011, a 9.0 magnitude earthquake struck the northeastern coast of Japan, triggering a devastating tsunami that swept away everything in its path.

Ishinomaki, the city where Sumi Abe and her grandson Jin Abe lived, was among the hardest hit.

When the tsunami hit, Sumi and Jin were in their home, which got buried by the debris.

For 9 days, the two survived in darkness, without water or food, eating yogurt and other items that remained in the refrigerator.

Jin eventually managed to get out through a gap in the rubble and alerted rescuers to his grandmother's location.

Sumi and Jin were rescued showing symptoms of hypothermia and were taken to a hospital.

Their survival story became a symbol of the strength and resilience of the Japanese people in the face of tragedy.

36

**Donny Dust, a professional caveman
who's making waves on TikTok.**

A master in primitive techniques, survival, and craftsmanship.

He has spent the last two decades surviving outdoors in the
world's most remote areas, such as the deserts of the Middle
East, the snow-covered mountains of North America, and the
jungles of Southeast Asia.

He now boasts 7.4 million followers on the social platform, and
in his videos, he teaches gadget-making techniques as they
would have been done thousands of years ago, as well as
survival methods that require no modern technology.

The caveman has a strong rapport with his followers and
responds to their requests.

They often ask him to make everyday objects or construct
shelters.

So far, he has managed to do it all using prehistoric tools like
bone or stone.

Donny Dust is 41 years old and served in the U.S. Armed Forces.

He currently teaches at Paleo Tracks Survival, a school in
Colorado where students attend to learn survival skills.

He has also been a consultant for TV series and films and
starred in 'Alone', a reality show that involves surviving alone in
a hostile environment.

37

During winter, it's best to avoid excessive sweating as sweat can cool the body and increase the risk of hypothermia.

Hypothermia occurs when the body temperature drops below normal (around 35 degrees Celsius) and can be a potentially life-threatening condition.

Sweating in the cold can also cause clothing to become damp, making it even harder to retain body heat.

Therefore, it's best to dress in layers and remove a layer if you start to sweat.

It's also important to stay properly hydrated and fed to maintain energy and body heat during the winter.

38

All parts of the dandelion are edible.

The young leaves can be used in salads and contain high amounts of vitamins A and C, as well as iron and calcium.

Dandelion flowers can also be eaten raw or cooked, and can be used to make tea or wine.

The roots can be roasted and used as a coffee substitute.

However, although the dandelion is edible and has some nutritional benefits, it also contains a high level of oxalic acid which can be harmful if consumed in large quantities.

Additionally, before consuming dandelions picked from the wild, it's important to ensure they haven't been exposed to pesticides or contamination.

39

Water is not the only source for staying well-hydrated.

In addition to water intake, electrolytes, such as sodium, potassium, magnesium, calcium, among others, are important for maintaining the body's fluid balance and preventing dehydration.

Electrolytes are responsible for maintaining cellular hydration and acid-base balance, as well as muscular and nerve function.

It's true that salty food can help replenish electrolytes, but they can also be obtained through sports drinks and oral rehydration solutions, like Pedialyte.

These solutions contain a mixture of water, sugar, and electrolytes that can help prevent or treat dehydration, especially in cases of gastrointestinal illness, diarrhea, or vomiting.

It's important to note that the amount of electrolytes needed varies based on individual needs and the physical activity performed.

It's recommended to speak with a healthcare professional before taking oral rehydration solutions, especially if one has an underlying health condition or is taking medications.

40

If you fall off a boat in open water, it's important to stay calm and assess the situation.

Instead of panicking and immediately starting to swim, try to find something that you can use as a floatation device, such as a lifejacket or some other nearby floating object.

If there's nothing within reach, then try to float in a horizontal position and keep your head out of the water to breathe.

Try not to exhaust your energy by swimming, as hypothermia and fatigue can decrease your chances of survival.

In such situations, it's important to maintain hope and try to attract the attention of rescue teams.

If you're with a group, try to keep everyone together and calm.

If you have an object that can be used to signal for help, like a flare or a mirror, use it to alert rescue teams.

You can also shout or wave your hands to get their attention.

It's important to remember that floating in a horizontal position in open water can be challenging due to currents and waves.

That's why wearing a lifejacket is essential for any boat trip.

Moreover, it's crucial to inform someone trustworthy about your sailing route and your estimated time of arrival, so in case of an emergency, they know where to look and can alert rescue teams promptly.

41

Pouring cold water or ice on the forearms to alleviate the effects of heat is known as a home remedy for hyperthermia or heatstroke.

Hyperthermia occurs when the body temperature rises too high, and it can be dangerous if not treated immediately.

Pouring cold water or ice onto the forearms is a method to cool the body quickly, as the forearms have large veins close to the skin and can cool the blood flowing through them.

This, in turn, can cool the body overall and alleviate symptoms of hyperthermia.

However, it's important to remember that this method is not a permanent solution and should not be used as a substitute for professional medical care if symptoms persist.

It's necessary to find a way to cool down properly, drink potable water, and, if needed, seek emergency medical attention if symptoms are severe.

42

It's important to carry a whistle when venturing into nature, as it's an effective way to attract attention and call for help in case of an emergency.

Unlike the human voice, the sound of a whistle can be heard over greater distances and doesn't wear out with time or fatigue.

The SOS signal with a whistle is an internationally recognized sound pattern consisting of three short blasts, followed by three long blasts, and another three short blasts, followed by a pause.

This pattern is repeated until help arrives.

It's vital to teach both children and adults venturing into the wilderness to carry a whistle and to use it appropriately, as it can save lives in emergency situations.

Moreover, it's important to keep the whistle in an accessible location and easy to reach, such as on a keychain or in a zippered pocket.

43

In some elevators, the symbol of a star may indicate the floor that provides the quickest route to the outside of the building.

The reason behind this is that when a building is constructed, building codes often require that at least one exit be easily accessible from within the building, typically through a set of stairs that lead directly outside.

The star button in some elevators is designed to take occupants directly to that level.

In an emergency situation, such as a fire, rapid access to an exit is crucial for safely and quickly evacuating the building.

However, it's important to note that not all buildings have this feature in their elevator, and in an emergency situation, it's recommended not to use the elevator but to use the stairs instead.

Furthermore, if you find yourself in an unfamiliar building, it's important to pay attention to emergency exits and plan an alternative evacuation route in case the elevator isn't a safe option.

44

Try to stay in your car if you get stuck in the snow.

Also, have an emergency kit in your car.

Hypothermia causes you to become delirious, and you might walk in the wrong direction and freeze to death.

Your car is also much easier to locate than you are.

It's advisable to keep in the car an unopened bottle of water, a blanket, matches, a wax candle, and a rope during the winter months.

The wax candle will provide enough heat to keep the car warm enough to survive when you wrap yourself in the blanket.

Tie the rope to the car if you go out to use the bathroom, so you can find your way back by following the rope if it's snowing.

45

It's good practice to be aware of exits in crowded places like concerts, stadiums, cinemas, theaters, shopping centers, and other public venues.

It's important to be prepared in case of an emergency, such as a fire, earthquake, or terrorist attack.

It's advisable to look for the emergency exit sign, which is typically marked in strategic and visible locations.

It's also important to pay attention to the instructions of the venue staff and follow their directions in the event of an emergency.

Moreover, it's advisable to plan an escape route in case there are multiple exits available.

It's best to choose the route that's furthest away from the crowd and that can ensure the quickest and safest exit.

46

Firstly, it's important to note that bees and wasps are different and have distinct behaviors when threatened.

Bees tend to be more docile and only attack when they feel threatened or to protect their hive.

Wasps, on the other hand, can be more aggressive and might attack without provocation.

In the case of bees, if you find yourself near a hive and feel they are starting to sting, it's important to run to a closed space, such as a building or a car.

Bees can't get into these places, and they will eventually leave the area.

For wasps, it's best to move away quickly and try to find a safe and enclosed space.

If there's no closed space available, try to cover your head and neck with thick clothing and run in a straight line as quickly as possible, avoiding sudden movements that might trigger more attacks.

In both cases, do not try to kill the bees or wasps as this can provoke more attacks and increase the danger.

If you've been stung, try to leave the area quickly and seek medical attention if you experience an allergic reaction or if you've been stung multiple times.

47

Crocodile Attack.

While it's true that crocodiles are fast in a straight line, and some wildlife experts recommend zigzagging and then running straight, there is no universally effective strategy to escape a crocodile.

In general, it's better to try and avoid contact with crocodiles in the first place, as they can be dangerous and aggressive.

If you are in an area where there are crocodiles, it's important to pay attention to warning signs and respect the animals' territory.

If a crocodile chases you, the best strategy is to run as fast as possible in a straight line, as crocodiles may be less agile on solid ground.

If possible, seek refuge in a high place, such as a tree or rock, and immediately call local authorities for help.

48

If you ever find yourself caught in a rip current, do not swim against it, as this will only exhaust you and leave you in the same position.

Instead, try to swim at an angle toward the shore in a direction perpendicular to the current.

This will allow you to gradually exit the current.

If you cannot escape the current, simply relax and float.

Once the current slows down or stops, you will be able to swim to the shore.

It's also important to remember to always swim in safe areas monitored by lifeguards and to obey water condition warning signs.

49

It's very important to keep your body warm and dry when in an outdoor survival situation, especially in extreme cold conditions.

To achieve this, it's necessary to construct a suitable shelter that protects you from the wind, rain, and snow.

However, even if you manage to build a good shelter, the cold and moisture from the ground can still affect your body temperature.

That's why it's important to make a proper bed inside the shelter.

You can use fern leaves, twigs, dry grass, moss, or any soft material you can find to create a thick insulating layer on the shelter floor.

This will help insulate your body from the cold ground and maintain body temperature.

It's also important to remember that the bed should be positioned far enough away from fire and other flammable objects inside the shelter.

Furthermore, ensure the bed is spacious and comfortable enough for you to sleep without experiencing pain or discomfort.

With a good bed, your body can rest and regain energy for the next day's activities.

50

The idea that floors 4 through 7 are the safest in a building or hotel is a theory that has circulated for years, but there is no solid evidence to back it up.

It's true that some security experts have recommended these floors as a good balance between safety and accessibility, as the lower floors are less likely to suffer damage in the event of earthquakes or explosions, and at the same time, higher floors might be more challenging to reach in case of a rapid evacuation.

However, there are also other factors that can influence safety, such as the building's location in relation to external danger sources, the quality of construction, and the safety measures implemented in the building.

It's important to remember that each situation is unique, and it's challenging to generalize about which floors are the safest in all cases.

In an emergency, it's essential to follow authorities' instructions and use common sense to assess the situation and make the best possible decisions to protect one's life and the safety of others.

51

It smells like smoke.

Surviving a house fire depends on your ability to escape quickly.

According to a study, frail individuals and those over 65 years of age are at the highest risk in home fires.

So, after installing smoke detectors on every floor, in bedrooms, and nearby areas, the next most critical survival step is to make an escape plan.

Once the smoke detector alarm sounds, you probably have only one or two minutes to get out.

In a smoke-filled room, the cleanest air is closer to the ground, so you should get low, staying as close to the floor as possible.

If you can't escape, place wet towels or bedding around the cracks in the doors.

52

A car accident.

No one emerges from the wrecked car, and help is miles away.

If you come across a car accident and decide to help, think about your personal safety first and assess the scene for safety.

Is the environment safe to approach?

Is the car on fire?

"Normally, you wouldn't want to move a victim, but you don't want the victim to be engulfed in flames."

-Massive bleeding: Look for blood spurting out with a bright red color. This suggests arterial bleeding. You'll want to stop the flow by compressing the blood vessel against the bone with direct pressure or with a tourniquet. Get a strip from a T-shirt and something rigid like a pen, a flashlight, or a stick; this will act as a windlass to tighten the tourniquet sufficiently.

-Airway: Check if the victim is breathing. If the victim is semi-conscious, lay them on their side so their tongue doesn't fall into their throat.

-Breathing: Check for anything that has impaled the chest. Use a plastic bag and adhesive tape, anything to cover those holes to prevent air from entering.

-Circulation: Address any other bleeding, like venous bleeding. Once I've taken care of the main things that the person could die from, I conduct a head-to-toe inspection to make sure I haven't missed anything.

-Hypothermia: With any trauma, body temperature drops. Cover the body with coats to retain body heat.

53

Your dog just ate an entire bar of chocolate.

The darker the chocolate, the more dangerous it is, due to the high amounts of theobromine.

Theobromine is a chemical cousin of caffeine that can accelerate the heart and raise blood pressure.

Even more toxic to dogs is xylitol, the sugar substitute found in many sugar-free gums.

When dogs consume it, this substance is quickly absorbed into the bloodstream and causes a strong release of insulin from the pancreas, leading to a drastic drop in blood sugar levels.

Save your pet:

Do not induce vomiting... sometimes it's not necessary; other times it can do more harm.

Oven and toilet cleaners, for example, are caustic and can damage the esophagus when coming back up.

If advised by a veterinarian, or if you're certain your dog has ingested xylitol or chocolate in the last 10 or 20 minutes, it is recommended to induce vomiting with hydrogen peroxide (the helpline will provide the correct dosage), which will irritate the stomach and make the dog vomit.

54

In situations where someone approaches you from behind, it can be difficult to determine whether the person is friendly or not.

It's important to maintain an alert and aware demeanor of your surroundings to be prepared for any situation.

Walking with your head held high is a good way to show that you're confident and conscious of your environment.

If you have a cane, giving it a quick spin can also be a way to deter someone from approaching you.

In general, it's advisable to trust your instincts and take steps to ensure your safety if you feel you're in danger.

55

You're alone, and you have food lodged in your throat.

According to the National Safety Council, around 5,000 people die from choking every year, with more than half being over the age of 74.

-Don't panic: If you can, breathe slowly and call 911. Even if you can't speak, the dispatcher should be able to recognize an emergency and send paramedics to your location.

-Cough forcefully: If something gets stuck in your throat, keep coughing vigorously to dislodge the object.

-Perform the Heimlich maneuver on yourself: If you can't remove the object by coughing and can't breathe, make a fist, place it just below the ribcage above the navel, grasp it with the other hand, and thrust inward and upward sharply. Do this 6 to 10 times quickly. Not working? Fall onto the edge of a low chair or couch to give a good force to expel the food. This has its risks, like breaking a rib, but if you're really turning blue, you have to do whatever it takes to dislodge the obstruction.

56

Someone fainted while working in the sun.

Heat-related illnesses can be life-threatening and come in stages:

-Heat cramps: Muscle cramps suggest dehydration. Take the victim to the shade and give them some water even if they're not thirsty. The cramps mean their electrolytes are low, so give them Gatorade diluted with water, as sports drinks tend to be high in sugar.

-Heat exhaustion: Profuse sweating is a big indicator of heat exhaustion, and this is serious. Move the victim to a cooler place, remove their hat, then unbutton their shirt and roll up the sleeves to allow cool air to lower their temperature. Have them sip water, not gulp it; you want to avoid vomiting.

-Heatstroke: The absence of sweat, bright red skin, a flushed face, lethargy, and difficulty speaking are all symptoms of heatstroke. This is a serious emergency. Apply cold compresses to the groin and underarms to lower the body temperature. Don't submerge the body in cold water, as that can jolt the heart out of rhythm...

57

I can't find the trail and it's getting dark.

Getting lost, even on a day hike, is quite common: there's an average of 11 search and rescue situations every day, according to the National Park Service.

Stay prepared:

-Date and time of departure and return.
-Location of the trailhead and names of trails, turning points, and GPS coordinates.
-Names of the people in your group.
-The gear you're carrying and the amount of food and water you have.

If you're lost in the woods, follow the S-T-O-P guidelines:

-Stop: as soon as you realize you might be lost, stop, stay calm, stay put. Don't wander aimlessly.

-Think: go over in your mind how you got to where you are. What trail markers should you be able to see?

-Observe: pull out your compass (you should have one on your smartphone) and determine your orientation based on where you're standing.
Do not proceed aimlessly. Consider retracing your steps, but only if you have a specific reason to take a step.

-Plan: most of the time the best move is to stay in place because it's more likely that searchers will find you. Moving just 0.6 miles increases the search area to almost 1 square mile.

Your survival priorities are shelter, water, food, and fire.

If you already have enough water or if you're cold and wet, shelter and fire may be more immediately important.

A person can succumb to hypothermia even at temperatures above 60 degrees in wet and windy conditions.

The body loses heat 25 times faster in cold water.

58

There are several techniques that can be used to purify and make water drinkable.

Some of the most common are:

-Boiling: boiling water is one of the easiest and most effective ways to purify it. It's important to boil the water for at least 5 minutes to kill any bacteria and viruses that may be present.

-Chlorination: adding a few drops of chlorine to the water can also kill bacteria and viruses. It's essential to follow the manufacturer's instructions to ensure you're using the correct amount of chlorine.

-Filtration: is another effective way to purify water. Special filters can be used to remove bacteria, viruses, and other contaminants. It's important to make sure the filter is designed to eliminate the specific contaminants found in the water.

-Distillation: is a process that involves evaporating the water and then condensing the steam to remove contaminants. It's an effective method but can be challenging to carry out in survival situations as it requires specialized equipment.

-UV rays: there are devices that emit UV rays to purify the water, eliminating bacteria, viruses, and other contaminants. However, this method is less effective if the water is murky or dirty.

It's crucial to understand that none of these techniques is entirely effective in all situations, and it's always best to treat water in multiple ways to increase the likelihood that it's safe to drink.

Moreover, it's essential to be wary of the water sources you use and avoid those that may be contaminated.

59

We must admit that we are lost.

Many people exacerbate the situation by refusing to admit they are lost.

They keep making assumptions and changing course, thinking they've found the right path.

In fact, a high percentage of people just keep going, hoping to find the correct way or a populated place.

This can lead things to get worse.

The problem with not knowing when to stop is that we might be moving away from safer areas.

If we venture into more secluded or remote areas, it will be much harder for rescue teams to find us.

So, what should we do?

The best thing is to admit that we are lost and set up camp in a clearing.

The fewer trees around, the higher the chances that rescue helicopters can spot us.

Often, it's best to give rescue teams time to do their job.

If the situation is very extreme and it seems there won't be any rescue, there will always be time to move later.

Another common mistake in survival situations is returning to the camp at night.

It's a typical way to get lost because in the dark everything looks different.

It's taking an unnecessary risk, and it's best to set up camp before it gets dark.

60

Hypothermia is a dangerous condition that occurs when the body's temperature drops significantly due to exposure to extreme cold.

If not treated properly, hypothermia can be fatal.

Some ways to combat it are:

–Seek shelter: If you find yourself in a hypothermic situation, the first thing you should do is seek shelter. A shelter can be a tent, an improvised refuge, or a cave. Protecting oneself from the wind and rain is crucial to prevent body heat loss.

–Keep the body dry: If you get wet, change out of your wet clothes into dry ones as soon as possible. This will reduce body heat loss.

–Warm the body: by using a thermal blanket, warm clothes, or hot water bags. If possible, share body heat with someone else.

–Consume warm food and drinks: this helps raise body temperature. Avoid alcohol as it can lower body temperature.

–Maintain physical activity: perform stretching exercises and gentle movements to increase blood circulation. Do not make abrupt or exhausting movements that could lead to a drop in body temperature.

–Seek medical help: if the symptoms of hypothermia are severe or if the affected person is unconscious, call emergency medical services immediately.

It's important to remember that prevention is the best way to combat hypothermia.

If you're going to be exposed to extreme cold, make sure you wear appropriate clothing to keep warm and dry, as well as be prepared for emergencies.

61

What not to do during a tornado?

One thing you should never do during a tornado is take shelter under a bridge.

You shouldn't do this even if you are in a vehicle and have managed to park underneath said bridge.

The reason is that tornadoes can cause the bridge to have a wind-tunnel effect.

This means that many debris flying from the tornado will pass underneath the bridge at hundreds of kilometers per hour.

These will be large projectiles, and you won't want to be in that place.

You should seek shelter, but in something that has a roof.

If it can be a basement, all the better.

What if we don't have any of that?

The best thing is to move away as fast as you can without looking back.

62

Elevator accidents are very rare, and elevators are designed with safety measures to minimize risks.

However, should an accident occur, it's important to stay calm and follow some safety tips.

First and foremost, if the elevator stops abruptly, do not try to force the doors open or attempt to exit on your own.

The elevator might not have reached a safe level yet, and opening the doors could be dangerous.

The best course of action is to press the emergency button or use the emergency phone inside the elevator to call for help.

You'll need to inform the elevator operator of your location and situation.

If the elevator stops and there's a gap between the floor and the elevator, don't try to exit or jump, as you might fall into the void.

Instead, try to get the attention of someone who can assist you from outside the elevator, or wait for emergency services to arrive.

As for the belief that one should jump before impact, this is incorrect and hazardous.

The impact can be very strong, and jumping will not reduce the force of the impact.

Lying down on the floor and spreading out the weight across the elevator's floor can help reduce injuries in the event of an accident, but the most important thing is to follow safety instructions and call for help immediately.

63

The human brain has a limited capacity to process information and tasks simultaneously.

When we focus on one task, like typing a text message, our brain redirects cognitive resources towards that activity, detracting from other tasks.

"Inattentional blindness" is a phenomenon where we become blind to significant stimuli in our environment because we're too focused on a specific task.

In the case of walking and texting, this can be particularly dangerous because we're distracted from our surroundings and might miss crucial danger signals.

For instance, we might not notice a red traffic light, an obstacle in our path, or an approaching car.

Moreover, walking while texting can affect balance and reaction time, increasing the risk of tripping or falling.

64

It's important to follow the safety instructions provided by the airline in the event of an emergency water landing.

Generally, the instructions include putting on the life vest before evacuating the plane, but if the cabin hasn't filled with water, it might be better to wait to inflate the vest.

If water begins to flood the cabin, it's crucial to swim towards the nearest exit as quickly as possible.

An inflated vest can make it harder to swim and escape the cabin.

Once you're outside the plane, you should inflate the vest to help you float and stay afloat while waiting to be rescued.

It's essential to follow the rescue personnel's instructions and not attempt to swim to shore unless it's within a reachable and safe distance.

65

The "Rule of 3" is a useful guide to remember the limits of the human body in extreme situations.

These are the limits typically referenced in the rule:

–3 minutes without air: A lack of air can cause irreversible brain damage and death within minutes. If you find yourself in a situation where you can't breathe, try to get out of danger as quickly as possible.

–3 hours without shelter in extreme weather conditions: In extremely cold or hot environments, it's vital to find shelter to protect oneself from the elements. Without it, you might suffer from hypothermia, heatstroke, or heat exhaustion.

–3 days without water: Water is essential for keeping the body hydrated and functioning. Without it, the kidneys and other organs might fail, which can be deadly within days.

–3 weeks without food: Although the body can survive without food for several weeks, a lack of nutrients can weaken the immune system and cause other health issues.

It's important to note that these are general guidelines, and each individual is different.

The time someone can survive without air, water, or food depends on many factors, such as age, health, and the environment they are in.

66

If cooking oil catches fire, one should avoid pouring water on the flames.

Instead, it's better to cover the pan with a lid, turn off the heat source, and let it cool down gradually.

Baking soda or a fire extinguisher can also be used to smother the flames.

It's important to exercise caution when handling hot oil and to have fire-extinguishing tools on hand in case of an emergency.

Additionally, it's recommended not to leave the kitchen unattended when cooking with oil and to have a fire extinguisher in the kitchen just in case.

67

The "+3/-8 Rule" is a general observation that most aviation accidents occur within the three minutes after takeoff and the eight minutes before landing.

This is because during these critical moments, the aircraft is in a high-energy phase and rapidly changes altitude, speed, and direction, which increases the risk of human errors or technical issues.

Takeoffs are particularly dangerous as the aircraft needs to reach the necessary speed to lift off and must navigate possible obstacles on the takeoff runway, such as birds or debris.

Landings are also risky since the aircraft is reducing its speed and altitude to touch down on a runway often limited in space and length.

However, it's important to note that the risk of being involved in an aviation accident remains very low compared to other modes of transportation.

Aircraft are designed to be safe and are equipped with multiple safety systems and redundancies.

Additionally, pilots and air traffic controllers are highly trained and adhere to stringent safety standards.

68

Learn the Swedish saying "Det finns inget dåligt väder, bara dåliga kläder".

"There's no bad weather, only bad clothing."

As a too-cool-for-school Scandinavian child refusing to wear his lovikkavantar (traditional hand-knitted mittens), this is probably a motto your grandmother would preach to you while you roll your eyes.

With a dose of optimism, two layers of long underwear, a thick parka, and one of those hats with earflaps, no snowstorm will stop you from enjoying the day.

69

Use gum wrappers and batteries.

Start a fire with a gum wrapper.

In the midst of a disaster, that pack of fruit-flavored gum serves a more significant need than just fighting hunger or freshening breath.

Cut a thin strip from a gum wrapper.

Fold the strip in half and cut diagonally across the folded strip.

When you unfold the strip, it should have a narrow point in the middle.

Hold the ends of the strip to the positive and negative ends of a battery.

Make sure the metallic side of the strip touches the battery, not the paper side, and you'll have a flame.

This method only works with wrappers that have a metallic side.

70

**In survival situations, it may be necessary
to construct traps to catch animals for food.**

Here are some common examples of traps:

–Snare trap: it works by wrapping a snare around a path used by the animal and adjusting it to its size. When the animal passes through the path, it will get caught in the snare, which will stop it and make it impossible to escape. It's important to note that some jurisdictions prohibit the use of snare traps, so you should make sure to research local laws before using this type of trap.

–Box trap: is a simple trap that consists of a box with a hinged door and bait inside. When the animal enters the box to investigate the bait, it steps on a trigger mechanism that closes the door behind it, trapping it.

–Pitfall trap: consists of a box with a door held in place by a lever. When the animal touches the lever to get food, the door releases and closes behind it, trapping it inside the box.

–Deadfall snare: works similarly to the snare trap, but instead of stopping the animal, it kills it immediately. Although effective, this type of trap can be dangerous and unethical, and some jurisdictions prohibit them.

It's important to remember that before using any trap, you should make sure to know the local laws and consider ethics and animal welfare.

It's also important to know how to prepare the meat of the trapped animal to prevent illnesses.

71

In a survival situation, a crucial skill to have is the ability to fish and source food from aquatic environments.

Below are some ways to construct fishing devices in survival situations:

-Fishing lines: This is the simplest and most common method of fishing in survival situations. All you need is a fishing line, a hook, and bait. The fishing line can be a string or fishing thread, while the bait can be anything from worms to pieces of meat. The hook can be improvised from wire or a nail.

-Fish traps: these are very effective and can be built in various ways. A common trap is the plastic bottle trap, where you cut a bottle in half and invert the top half inside the bottom half. Make a small opening at the edge and place bait inside. Fish can enter but cannot exit.

-Fishing nets: can be highly effective in catching large quantities of fish. Fishing nets can be improvised with any fabric or mesh that has holes small enough to retain fish. The fabric can be attached to sticks or branches to create a structure, then placed in the water with weights to keep it in place.

-Harpoons: are very effective for catching large fish in survival situations. A harpoon can be improvised from a stick or branch, with a sharp tip on one end and a rope on the other. The harpoon is thrown at the fish, then pulled in using the rope.

-Crab traps: are very effective for catching crustaceans and other aquatic animals. They can be built in various ways, but a common method is to use a mesh or fabric to create a bag with an opening at one end. The bag is filled with bait and placed in the water with weights to keep it in place. Crabs and other animals can enter but cannot exit.

It's essential to remember that in most survival situations, you need a fishing license to fish legally.

Furthermore, it's always crucial to follow conservation and fishing laws in your area to prevent harming the aquatic ecosystem.

72

Dew collection.

It's an effective way to obtain water in survival situations.

In addition to the fabric technique, there are other ways to collect dew.

One option is to use clean glass or plastic containers, placed in areas where dew forms overnight.

By morning, the dew will have condensed on the container's walls, and it can be collected with a clean cloth or poured directly into a container for drinking.

Another way to collect dew is by using plants with large leaves, like lilies or banana plants.

You can place a clean plastic bag over the leaf and secure it with a rubber band or string.

Overnight, dew will accumulate on the leaf and inside the bag, and can be carefully collected into a clean container.

It's important to note that the collected dew should be treated before consumption to eliminate any potential contamination.

The most effective way to sterilize the water is by boiling it for at least 10 minutes.

If boiling the water isn't possible, it can be treated with purification tablets or portable water filters.

73

The transpiration technique.

It's a method to collect water in nature when no other sources are available.

It involves covering a leafy branch of a plant with a plastic bag, in such a way that the bag captures the plant's natural transpiration, which is the process by which the plant loses water through evaporation from its leaves.

To collect the water, first find a plant with fresh and healthy leaves, preferably in a sunny area.

Then, place a clear plastic bag over a leafy branch, making sure the bag is tightly sealed and there are no air leaks.

Tie the ends of the bag securely around the branch, so the bag stays in place and forms a sealed air pocket around the leaves.

During the day, sunlight will heat the air inside the bag, causing water to evaporate from the plant's leaves and condense on the interior surface of the bag.

The water will then accumulate at the bottom of the bag, where you can collect and drink it.

It's important to note that not all plants are suitable for water collection through transpiration, and some plants can even be toxic.

Furthermore, make sure the plastic bag you use is sturdy and hole-free to prevent water contamination.

74

Improvised Compass.

Most people venturing into the wilderness carry a compass, but if you find yourself lost and without one, you could create a water puddle or use the water you have and place it in a container, waiting for the water to settle.

Now, you can gently place a leaf on the water and a metal needle or a straightened piece of wire (rub it against your clothing to magnetize it) on top of it.

The Earth's magnetic field will slowly align the needle along the north-south line.

Another way to make an improvised compass is to use a large sheet of aluminum foil, a magnetized needle, and some water.

First, place the aluminum foil sheet on a flat surface and put the magnetized needle in the center of the sheet.

Then, pour a bit of water onto the aluminum foil, right around the needle.

Ensure that the needle floats freely in the water and doesn't touch the edges of the aluminum foil.

The needle will point towards the magnetic north pole, allowing you to determine the cardinal north direction.

75

The sun can be a useful tool for determining directions in survival situations or when in unfamiliar areas.

To use the sun's rising position to determine directions, consider the following:

-In spring and autumn: during these equinoxes, the sun rises approximately in the east and sets in the west. So if you stand facing the sun at sunrise, the east will be right where the sun is rising, the west will be behind you, the south will be to your right, and the north will be to your left.

-In summer: during the summer solstice, the sun rises more towards the northeast and sets more towards the northwest. If you stand facing the sun at sunrise, the east will be slightly to the right from the direction where the sunrise is seen, the west will be slightly to the left, the south will be behind you, and the north will be in front of you.

-In winter: during the winter solstice, the sun rises more towards the southeast and sets more towards the southwest. If you stand facing the sun at sunrise, the east will be slightly to the left from where the sun rises, the west will be slightly to the right, the south will be in front of you, and the north will be behind you.

It's important to note that these are just rough estimates and the sun's exact position can vary slightly depending on geographical location and time of day.

Additionally, it's recommended to use other navigation methods in conjunction with the sun's position, such as using a compass, maps, natural landmarks, and observing the stars.

76

Burning herbs to ward off mosquitoes and other insects is an ancient technique that has been used in many cultures around the world.

Some herbs, such as rosemary, thyme, or mint, contain chemical compounds that have repellent properties for insects.

When these herbs are burned, the chemical compounds are released into the air and can deter insects.

In addition to the herbs mentioned, other plants and substances, such as eucalyptus, cedar, camphor, and citronella, can also be burned as they also have insect-repelling properties.

Essential oils or scented candles containing these extracts can also be used.

However, it's important to note that burning herbs can produce smoke, which may be irritating to some people and is not recommended for those with respiratory issues.

Furthermore, burning herbs can be dangerous if not done with caution, especially in windy areas or where flammable materials are nearby.

77

The position of the moon in the night sky can be useful for navigation, but it's important to keep in mind that the position and shape of the moon change constantly throughout its monthly cycle.

Furthermore, the moon's position cannot provide precise orientation in terms of north, south, east, and west.

However, there are some general guidelines one can follow.

For instance, if the moon is high in the sky, it's likely late in the night and, therefore, the east is likely behind you and the west in front.

If the moon is near the horizon, it's probably early in the night with the east in front of you and the west behind.

It's also possible to use the position of the stars for general orientation.

For example, the North Star, also known as Polaris, is always in the northern celestial hemisphere and can be used to determine the northern direction.

In any case, it's important to bear in mind that navigating in low light conditions can be challenging, and it's best to be prepared with a compass, maps, and other navigation equipment before venturing into unfamiliar terrain.

78

Escaping from handcuffs.

Most standard handcuffs can be picked with a hairpin, a clip, or a piece of wire.

If you're using a hairpin, make sure to scrape off the plastic tip from one of the ends.

The steps are as follows:

-Straighten out the metal of the tool you're using, whether it's the hairpin, clip, or wire piece.

-Insert the pin halfway into the handcuff lock and bend it to form a 90-degree angle.

-Insert the pin fully into the keyhole and bend it in the opposite direction. As a tip, the end should resemble the letter "Z".

-This bent pin should act as a key, insert it into the keyhole and wiggle it around. If done correctly, the pin should lift the locking mechanism and unlock the device. Be patient, as it might take some time.

Double-locking handcuffs can also be opened using the same technique.

79

Aron Ralston: Flesh Against Rock.

Skillfully and graphically brought to the big screen by Danny Boyle in "127 Hours," the five days Aron Ralston spent alone and trapped in a tiny crevice of Blue John Canyon (near Moab, Utah) transformed him from a fairly modest mountaineer to a one-armed celebrity in the United States.

It was in 2003, while trekking an area he knew intimately, that a rock dislodged as he used it for support. It fell, pinning his arm mercilessly against the canyon wall.

The mistakes Aron made came back to haunt him.

Confident in his abilities and, as he admitted, thinking of himself as quite tough, he had decided there was no need to inform anyone of his plans.

He carried no communication device, had minimal provisions—just enough for a day's exertion—and little more than a liter of water.

There was no way to free his arm, no means to get more food or water, and no hope of anyone finding him.

He tried to create a pulley system with the rock, attempted to carve it with a nearly useless knife, depleted his water and then his urine, exhausted his strength and the battery of his video camera (recording hours of his misery, including a farewell to his parents).

To survive the night's temperatures, he wrapped ropes around his torso and legs... and eventually carved his name and presumed date of death on one of the claustrophobic walls enclosing him.

After 5 days, amidst deliriums and hallucinations, with a dull blade which Ralston described as "the kind you'd get free with a flashlight," he managed to amputate his own arm without bleeding out or fainting, still maintaining enough strength to walk the nearly thirty kilometers back to his car and confront a 20-meter rappel.

He eventually encountered a European couple and their child, who alerted the rescue services.

80

Beck Weathers: The Worst Day on Everest.

Weathers was an experienced 49-year-old American climber, but nothing he had faced before was going to prepare him for that spring of '96.

On May 10th, amidst the confusion of an unexpected storm that exacerbated mistakes like the overcrowding of climbers at steps such as the Hillary Step, and the late hour at which some mountaineers were reaching the summit, Rob Hall, the leader of one of the commercial expeditions on Everest, made a distressing radio report, stating among other things, the death of Beck Weathers.

On the 11th, Beck's body was found next to that of the Japanese climber Yasuko Namba, both eroded by ice and snow, with only part of the face and right hand visible.

He was still faintly breathing, but due to his comatose state and the impossibility of moving him from that location, his death was again confirmed.

No one had ever woken up from a hypothermic coma before, and if they did, in what condition would they be to move on their own?

Science might have its explanations, but Beck woke up:

"At first, I thought it was a dream. When I came to, I thought I was in bed. I didn't feel cold; I didn't feel anything. I opened my eyes and saw my right hand in front of my face. Then I noticed how frozen it was, and that jolted me. Eventually, I woke up enough to realize I was screwed and that the cavalry wasn't coming to rescue me, so I had to get myself together."

After 30 hours buried on the mountain, hearing various teammates or rescue teams pronounce him dead, his brain suddenly came alive again.

Finally, nearly 6 hours after awakening, the American showed up at the medical tent of the third high camp, numb and with grotesque frostbite.

He stayed there for the following hours, during which a blizzard tore apart the tent, forcing him to spend another night exposed and partially suffocated by the canvas.

The next morning, no one could believe he had survived again.

81

Descent into Hell.

A small British flag flutters in the thin air at nearly 7,300 meters where it stands.

Chris Bonington and Doug Scott, two pioneers of vertical dream, have climbed up to this point.

They didn't summit just any mountain: they've trodden on the Ogre, a fang of the Karakoram with oceanic walls upon which no foot had ever stepped.

It was July 17, 1977, and two of their companions, Mo Anthoine and Clive Rowland, had exhausted their energies before the final assault.

Therefore, Bonington and Scott embarked on a grueling 15-hour uninterrupted ascent to overcome the upper bastions of this stark and misty Baintha Brakk.

During the first rappel, Doug Scott suffers a fall they try to remedy with a recovery pendulum.

During this maneuver, he makes another mistake, crashing into the rocks.

He fractures both ankles and shatters the lenses of his glasses above 7,000 meters.

With slim chances of getting off the mountain, the two climbers begin a slow and agonizing descent that would last for seven days.

Due to their prolonged absence, the rest of the expedition assumes them dead and starts to withdraw from the slopes.

Scott persists in his languid escape: he tears his kneecaps and wrists, moving like a rag doll.

Moreover, the mountain hasn't had its last say, unleashing a two-day storm that forces them to take shelter in an ice cave.

As a result, Bonington contracts pneumonia, and in his weakened and imprecise state, suffers an accident, breaking a couple of ribs.

Despite everything, and with the support of Mo Anthoine and Clive Rowland in the final stages of the descent, they reach base camp where they had already been mourned as lost.

On the brink of their energy, they finally see the rescue helicopter approaching.

And just when it seems everything is over, the chopper plunges into the void with them inside, luckily with no casualties.

82

Poon Lim.

Lim was 25 years old when he enlisted on the SS Ben Lomond, a British vessel, amidst the boiling tensions of World War II, towards the end of 1942.

Just days after setting sail, the merchant ship was ambushed by the fire of a German submarine and quickly sank, taking over 50 souls with it, a few hundred miles off the coast of Brazil.

Poon Lim had just enough time to grab a lifejacket, jump into the sea, and survive the suction of the tangled mass of iron and blood that the Ben Lomond had become.

Of the crew, only five other sailors survived, but they were captured by the crew of the German submarine while still struggling to stay afloat in the Atlantic waters.

The young Asian man managed to reach one of the emergency lifeboats, measuring 3 by 3 meters.

Inside the raft, he found a minuscule survival kit intended to support a small group for a couple of days.

Its contents included: eight cans of biscuits, a barrel with 30 liters of water, a couple of chocolate bars, some sugar lumps, a few flares, two aluminum cans, and a flashlight.

However, the raft had no oars, sails, or any other propulsion system, leaving him adrift endlessly, his fate at the mercy of the unpredictable waves, and exposed to the sun and wind.

By the fourth and fifth week, he faced his biggest challenge: surviving without provisions. So, he fashioned a hook from pieces of the flashlight and used his last biscuit as bait.

His first catch was a sardine, which he used to lure larger prey.

On one occasion, he filled the entire boat with his catch, but the amount of viscera and dead fish forced him to throw some overboard, which in turn attracted all sorts of sharks.

Reduced to his primitive needs, water became his next concern during a drought that interrupted his regular rainwater collection.

To quench his thirst, he lured an albatross to his raft and killed it with his teeth.

Soon after, an aerial squadron canceled his rescue due to weather conditions, and an American cargo ship passed by him, only to abandon him to his fate after verifying his nationality.

On April 5, 1943, a Brazilian fishing boat responded to his distress signals.

He had drifted more than 1,000 kilometers.

83

Mike Couillard.

In early 1995, Mike and his son Matt were skiing at the Kartalkaya resort, set amidst the robust Turkish landscapes of Koroglu.

As the night was about to fall over the mountains, father and son decided to make one last, treacherous descent before returning to the warmth of the fireplace.

A howling blizzard, a misjudged route, and an unfamiliar forest would eventually lead the two into disorientation and a subsequent week of nightmare.

Mike's first concern, understandably, was for his son.

He built a makeshift shelter using their skis and surrounding foliage, ensuring that Matt kept warm.

They would spend three days, barely shielded by their bivouac, waiting for a rescue that wouldn't come during one of the worst storms ever to hit the region.

Without food, fire, and only the water they could melt, the hours wore down their spirits, resigning them to accept their fate.

During those days, a hundred volunteers combed the mountains, but after days of searching in increasingly challenging conditions, they gave up, presuming the duo had perished.

They had been huddled under the branches that served as their ceiling for a week when a break in the storm allowed them to take a look outside.

At that moment, Mike, using what little strength he had left, managed to climb higher up the mountain and spotted what he believed to be cabins in a blurred horizon.

He was about to make a life-altering decision.

He removed his warm clothing, handed it to his son, and trudged forward, drained and alone, like a robot on a mission, leaving Matt behind, waiting for the uncertain prospect of help.

Indeed, there were cabins where he had first set his sights and hopes.

However, they were deserted.

The night he spent within those empty walls must have been utterly crushing.

Had he left his son for nothing? The answer came the next morning in the form of Turkish loggers, van included.

84

The Wild Boars.

After a soccer practice in June 2018, 12 members of a Thai soccer team and their coach decided to explore the nearby Tham Luang cave, one of the longest in Thailand.

The boys, aged between 11 and 16, and their 25-year-old coach, waded into the waters and began exploring the cave.

When a sudden flood occurred, they ventured deeper, reaching a raised platform, 4 kilometers inside the cave system.

The flood filled the winding cave system with water, trapping the boys for 17 days.

For the first 9 days, they had no food and relied on dripping stalactites for water, but they didn't just sit and wait.

Realizing they were trapped, the boys took turns digging a nearly 5-meter hole in the cave wall, hoping to find an exit.

They meditated to conserve energy and avoid thinking about food.

Then, British divers, who had set out from the cave's entrance 3 hours earlier, stumbled upon the boys.

Over the course of a 3-day mission, the divers retrieved each player and their coach.

Tragically, a former Thai Navy Seal lost his life during the rescue efforts.

85

Ángela Hernández.

In July 2018, Ángela Hernández was driving near Big Sur on Highway 1, heading to Southern California in her SUV, when a small animal crossed the road.

Hernández swerved to avoid it, and in doing so, her SUV veered off the road, plummeting about 60 meters down a cliff to a desolate and rocky beach.

She suffered a brain hemorrhage, broken ribs, a broken collarbone, ruptured blood vessels in both eyes, and a collapsed lung, but she didn't die.

When she came to, water was up to her knees.

She broke the window with a multi-tool, crawled through it, swam to the beach, and passed out.

When she regained consciousness, she had no shoes and was understandably battered, but she began walking along the shoreline looking for help.

She used a hose from her car to collect water dripping from moss on the shoreline and walked for days.

From where she was, she could see cars passing above the cliff, but they couldn't see or hear her screams.

It wasn't until hikers, exploring the beach looking for fishing spots, stumbled upon her wrecked Jeep and scoured the beach until they found Hernández curled up sleeping on some rocks.

86

Steven Callahan.

After successfully crossing the Atlantic solo in his 6.5-meter sloop, Callahan set out on his return journey in January of 1981.

The storm that engulfed his boat one night didn't worry him, but the hole that a whale or shark made in the hull of his boat during the storm did.

As the boat began to sink, Callahan repeatedly dove into the sinking ship to retrieve survival equipment.

With food and water for a few days, Callahan got into his 1.80-meter circular raft, adrift, almost 1,300 kilometers west of the Canary Islands and slowly drifting further away.

Callahan fished with a spear and sourced water using a solar still.

On day 14, he signaled a passing ship, but they didn't see him.

After 1 month, he drifted out of shipping routes.

By day 50, he was covered in saltwater sores, battling dehydration in tropical waters, and striving to patch a hole in his raft.

Exhausted, and after losing a third of his body weight, Callahan was finally spotted by fishermen off the coast of Guadeloupe, as birds and fish circled his raft, seeking the fish innards he was throwing into the sea.

He had been adrift for 76 days.

87

The Robertson Family.

For 38 days, the Robertson family was lost at sea.

Patriarch Dougal Robertson, a British dairy farmer, simply wanted to take his family on a boat trip.

On January 27, 1971, Dougal, his wife, and their 4 children embarked on a wooden schooner named Lucette, headed for unknown destinations.

Douglas, the eldest son, told the BBC that his father had made few preparations for the journey, even though he had been in the British merchant navy.

For 17 months at sea, the family fared well, sailing from port to port and seeing the world.

But on June 15, 1972, the family encountered a pod of killer whales off the coast of the Galápagos Islands.

The whales attacked the boat, splintering it and causing severe damage.

The boat was taking on water, and all they had was a lifeboat and a small dinghy, with food for only 6 days.

They survived on rainwater and hunting turtles, drifting at sea, hoping to navigate the Pacific currents until reaching the ocean's center, which would push them towards America.

After 16 days, the raft was no longer usable, so the family fled to a dinghy.

It was a 3-meter vessel and they were well over its capacity, but they managed to hang on until they were discovered by Japanese fishermen on July 23, 1972.

88

Harrison Okene.

On May 28, 2013, divers working on the wreckage of the Jackson-4 were attempting to triage the vessel, which lay 30 meters off the coast of Nigeria after capsizing.

What they didn't expect to find was a survivor.

Harrison Okene was the ship's cook.

He was in the restroom when the ship overturned, and he tried to reach an emergency exit hatch but couldn't make it.

Water began to flood the vessel with Okene trapped inside.

In the end, he found himself trapped with a one-square-meter air pocket.

After 3 days, he had lost hope, but then he heard a knock.

It was the hammer of the divers working on the ship's surface.

Eventually, they supplied him with diving equipment and took him to a decompression chamber, where he had to spend 2 days.

He had been at depths that should have killed him, in a situation that claimed the lives of everyone else on board.

As expected, he vowed never to go out to sea again.

89

Ernest Shackleton.

This man had challenged the South Pole once before, and in 1914, he was ready to face it again, setting off with a group of 28 men.

They hoped to cross the icy continent and reach a ship waiting for them on the other side.

However, they became trapped in the ice as their ship, the Endurance, began to crumble.

Eventually, supplies began to dwindle, and the men took to their lifeboats, drifting to an island, a journey that took them 14 days through the treacherous Antarctic seas.

From there, they had to mount another expedition to South Georgia Island, the nearest inhabited island, almost 1,600 kilometers from their original starting point.

Despite the myriad challenges, all 28 men on the mission survived, though some of the dogs weren't so fortunate and were eaten as food supplies ran out.

The ship waiting on the other side of Antarctica, the Ross Sea Party, wasn't so lucky, suffering 3 deaths.

90

Juliane Koepcke.

On Christmas Eve of 1971, Koepcke boarded LANSA Flight 508.

The plane was struck by lightning and began to disintegrate in mid-air.

Koepcke, still strapped to her seat, found herself plummeting nearly 4,000 meters above the Peruvian jungle.

When she regained consciousness, she was bruised all over and had a broken collarbone.

However, she was alive and the sole survivor of the flight, leaving her alone in the jungle.

Her only food was a candy, but she found a small stream and submerged herself in it, managing to stay hydrated.

The jungle insects constantly tormented her, but they didn't consume her alive.

Maggots infected her arm, but after nine days, she stumbled upon a camp.

She administered some rudimentary first aid to herself, including pouring gasoline over the maggot infection.

A few hours later, some lumber workers found her, gave her first aid, and took her to an inhabited area, from where she was airlifted to a hospital.

Her story was recounted in the documentary "Wings of Hope" (2000) by director Werner Herzog, who had a seat reserved on that very flight before canceling it at the last moment.

91

Ada Blackjack.

Ada Blackjack, an Alaskan native, was a member of the Indigenous Iñupiat people.

She was hired by Canadians Vilhjalmur Stefansson and Allan Crawford for an expedition to the Wrangel Islands, which are now considered Russian territory.

The objective was to claim them in the name of Canada, and Blackjack served as the expedition's seamstress and cook.

Five expedition members stayed on the island on September 16, 1921, as a territorial claim, but their rations soon ran out.

Three members left in search of help while Blackjack cared for an ailing crew member, who later perished, leaving her alone on the island.

Blackjack survived there for 2 years, a formidable feat given the risk of polar bear attacks.

She learned to hunt seals and survived partly on their meat until she was finally rescued on August 28, 1923, nearly 2 years after being left on the island.

According to a webpage from the University of Alaska-Anchorage, Blackjack did not receive a hero's welcome.

Instead, she faced criticism for not having saved the life of her crewmate, although the family eventually vindicated her after reuniting with her and releasing a statement claiming that Blackjack had done everything possible to save their son's life.

Nevertheless, she spent the rest of her life in poverty before passing away in 1983.

92

Following a flowing watercourse downstream can be a good strategy to find civilization or assistance if lost in the wilderness.

However, this strategy is only effective if followed with caution and certain considerations.

The first thing is to ensure the water is flowing in the right direction.

Sometimes, the water might be flowing in the opposite direction due to an obstacle in its path, such as a dam or a mountain.

Moreover, it's important to note that following a river's course can lead us down challenging and dangerous paths.

Rivers can have strong currents, rapids, waterfalls, and deep pools that can be hazardous if one doesn't have the appropriate skills and equipment.

Another consideration is that human settlements aren't always directly located on the watercourse.

Sometimes, they might be at some distance or in a different direction.

Therefore, it's essential to be on the lookout for signs or traces of human activity, such as trails, roads, structures, or smoke.

93

Carrying certain items in the car can be very useful in case of an emergency.

-Water: It is essential for human survival and it's important to have it on hand in case you get stranded or lost.
It's recommended to carry at least 3 liters of water per person.

-Non-perishable and high-caloric foods like nuts: In the event of getting stuck or lost, it's essential to have foods that won't spoil and are high in calories to maintain energy. Nuts are a good option as they're rich in healthy fats and proteins.

-A flashlight: Necessary if you get trapped or lost in the dark. It's vital to have a light source to see and move safely.

-A first-aid kit: In the event of an accident or injury, a first-aid kit can be crucial for providing initial care until professional help arrives.

-A blanket: Can be handy in cold weather or for sun protection. It can also be used to help retain body heat in an emergency.

-A mobile phone charger: Helpful to keep the phone charged in case you need to call for emergency assistance or ask for help.

-Matches: Useful for lighting a fire for cooking or staying warm.

-Iodine tincture: Can be used to disinfect wounds and prevent infections in case of injury. It can also be used to purify water if necessary.

It's important to remember that these items can be of great assistance, but it's equally essential to learn how to use them and be prepared for emergency situations.

94

In the event of a plane crash, the primary priority is the safety and survival of the people involved.

If one survives the accident, it's important to assess the situation and take steps to increase the chances of being rescued.

It's true that staying near or by the plane can be beneficial for being located by rescue teams.

The wreckage of the plane is a clear signal for search teams, and survivors can use parts of the aircraft to build shelters or signals to draw the attention of rescuers.

However, in some cases, it might be necessary to move away from the plane to seek help or resources.

It's important to note that the decision to stay near the plane should depend on the individual situation.

If the location of the plane is dangerous or doesn't provide resources for survival, then it might be necessary to look for a safer place or where one can find resources like water, food, and shelter.

In general, it's crucial to be prepared for emergency situations and have basic survival knowledge to increase the chances of surviving in the event of an accident.

Additionally, it's recommended to follow the instructions of the airline staff in case of an emergency and pay attention to safety measures before the flight.

95

Bear Grylls.

He is a British survival expert, adventurer, and television presenter.

He is best known for his television programs, such as "Man vs. Wild" (known as "Born Survivor" in the UK), in which he showcases his survival skills in various hostile environments around the world.

He has also appeared in other television shows like "The Island with Bear Grylls" and "Running Wild with Bear Grylls," where he takes celebrities to remote areas and challenges them to survive.

In addition to his TV shows, Bear Grylls has authored several books on survival and adventure, including "Bear Grylls' Survival Guide," "Adventures in the Mountains," and "The Art of Extreme Survival."

He is also a prominent charity activist and serves as an ambassador for several charitable organizations and foundations.

Grylls is renowned for his survival skills, such as the ability to build makeshift shelters, find water and food in the wild, and create fire without tools.

He has also accomplished various adventure feats, including climbing several mountains worldwide and navigating the Atlantic Ocean in an inflatable boat.

96

When we find ourselves lost in nature, one of the oldest and most effective ways to navigate is by using the stars.

Some tips and techniques for navigating with the stars in a survival situation:

-Learn to identify the stars: Before heading out into the wilderness, it's important to know how to identify some of the main stars and constellations. The most recognized constellations include the Big Dipper, Little Dipper, Orion, and Cassiopeia.

-Locate the celestial north pole: If you're in the northern hemisphere, the North Star points towards the celestial north pole, helping you with orientation. If you're in the southern hemisphere, the Southern Cross points towards the celestial south pole.

-Determine direction: Once you've located the celestial north pole, you can use it to figure out direction. Facing the North Star and stretching out your arms, your right hand will point east and the left hand will point west. The opposite direction will be south.

-Observe star movement: If you can't locate the North Star, you can also watch the movement of stars to determine direction. In the northern hemisphere, stars move clockwise around the North Star, while in the southern hemisphere, they move counterclockwise around the Southern Cross.

-Use a compass: If you have a compass with you, you can use it to complement your star-based navigation. Ensure the compass is level and its needle points to the magnetic north.

97

The moon can be a useful tool for survival, especially for navigation at night.

-The moon as a compass: if you have a watch, you can use the moon to determine north and south. If you're in the northern hemisphere, look for the moon and draw an imaginary line from its position down to the horizon. The midpoint of that line will be approximately south. If you're in the southern hemisphere, look for the moon and draw a line from its position to the horizon, the midpoint of that line will be approximately north.

-Use the moon for orientation: The shape of the moon can help you determine the time of day and the direction you are moving in. If the moon is a crescent, is near the horizon, and its curved side points west, it means it's early in the evening and east is behind you. If the moon is a crescent with its curved side pointing east, it's close to dawn and west is behind you.

-Use the moon to light your way: The moon's light can be helpful for moving at night without the need for a flashlight. If the moon is full or near full, its light might be enough to walk on trails and paths without tripping. Additionally, the moon's light can be helpful to avoid being detected by nocturnal predators, as many of them can't see in total darkness.

Overall, the moon can be a valuable tool for survival, as long as you know how to use it.

98

The Right Backpack.

It's a fundamental item for survival in dangerous situations or adventure trips in the wilderness.

Among the items that should be carried in the backpack to ensure survival are a small, water-resistant flashlight or a headlamp, along with spare batteries for the light.

It's also crucial to carry waterproof matches and a lighter to be able to start a fire for warmth or cooking food.

Furthermore, it's recommended to carry enough water, at least 1 gallon (3.8 liters) per person for each day, as well as non-perishable food and a manual can opener for canned foods.

It's essential to have a first-aid kit and a sharp knife for cutting food and materials that might be needed.

Choosing a well-thought-out route is also crucial for survival, especially when in danger.

Therefore, it's important to have a map and a compass in the backpack and know how to use them.

You can also carry a GPS for orientation, though it's not always reliable.

In general, good planning and preparation before heading out on a wilderness adventure can make all the difference in emergency situations.

99

Tides.

They can have a significant impact on survival, especially for those on the coast or at sea.

The tide is the periodic change in sea level that occurs due to the gravitational pull of the moon and sun on Earth.

These tidal forces can create dangerous currents and significant changes in water levels, which can complicate navigation and fishing.

There are several types of tides, which occur depending on the relative position of the moon and the sun, as well as local topography.

Some of the most common types of tides are:

–High tide: The water level rises and reaches its highest point. High tides can flood coasts and make navigation difficult in certain areas.

–Low tide: The water level drops and reaches its lowest point. Low tides can expose dangerous rocks and obstacles and make navigation challenging in certain areas.

–Neap tide: This happens when the moon and sun are at right angles to each other, and the gravitational pull of both celestial bodies cancels each other out. As a result, tides are less extreme, and there are fewer currents.

–Spring tide: This happens when the moon and sun are aligned, and the gravitational pull of both celestial bodies adds together. As a result, tides are more extreme, and there are stronger currents.

It's crucial for sailors, fishermen, and others working at sea to be aware of tidal conditions and prepare adequately for them.

Additionally, it's essential to follow the recommendations of tide experts and avoid any dangerous activities during extreme high and low tides.

100

A strong blow to the head.

It can have severe and even fatal consequences if not handled properly.

Immediately after the blow, it's important to check for signs of concussion, such as dizziness, headache, memory loss, nausea, and vomiting.

If these symptoms are present, seek medical attention right away.

Furthermore, as indicated in the information provided, it's important to note that even if you initially seem fine after a blow to the head, if you later experience an unusual feeling of fatigue, weakness, or confusion, seek medical attention right away.

This could be a sign that a clot is forming, and urgent measures may be needed to prevent more severe consequences.

In general, it's recommended to be cautious and seek medical attention if a blow to the head occurs, especially if there's a loss of consciousness, persistent vomiting, seizures, or if the affected person has trouble speaking or walking.

In an emergency, immediately call emergency services or go to the nearest emergency room.

101

If a nuclear bomb drops, it's crucial to act quickly to minimize the effects of radiation.

First, you should seek shelter in a building as soon as possible.

Ideally, you should look for a multi-story concrete or brick building or one with a basement, as these materials offer better protection against radiation.

Once inside the building, head to the basement or the central part of the building.

This helps increase the distance between yourself and the radioactive materials outside.

It's vital to stay in the shelter until authorities say it's safe to leave.

To further protect against nuclear radiation, take additional measures.

Walls, ceilings, and floors can help block radiation, so stay inside a building for as long as possible.

You should also close all windows, doors, and any other openings that might allow radiation to enter.

Furthermore, cover your mouth and nose with a cloth or mask to prevent inhaling radioactive particles.

If possible, seek shelter in a basement or underground structure, as the earth also provides some protection against radiation.

In general, it's best to follow the instructions of the authorities and have an emergency plan in case of a potential nuclear attack.

It's also essential to know the warning signs and be prepared to act swiftly in an emergency.

If you've enjoyed our survival book for the outdoors and urban areas, we'd love for you to share your experience on Amazon.

We know that in emergency situations, survival information and skills can mean the difference between life and death.

Sharing your feedback is very valuable to us and can help others learn more about how to survive in hostile environments, as well as enjoy the reading experience.

Your review also helps us improve and create more useful content for our readers.

We understand that writing a review can be time-consuming, but we ask that you take a few minutes of your time to share your thoughts and opinions.

Your support is vital to us and motivates us to continue working to provide the best possible content for our readers.

Thank you for your support, and we hope this book has provided you with insightful information on surviving in both nature and the city!

★ ★ ★ ★ ★